W9-BUC-449

1842

FIRST AMERICAN COMICS

2014

Copyright © Leopold Publishing – august 2014

INTRODUCTION

This is a facsimile of the first American comic book ever published. It has been first printed in Manhattan, New York City, in 1842. Actually, it was a pirated version of the first comic book ever published in the world, authored and drawn by famous Swiss novelist, caricaturist and cartoonist, Rodolphe Töpffer (1799-1846). Today, Töpffer is unanimously considered as "the father of comic strips". So the original version of this story is "Les Amours de Monsieur Vieuxbois", and it was first published a few years earlier in Geneva, Switzerland, in 1837.

The title drawn by Rodolphe Töpffer for the cover of the
first printing of "Les Amours de Monsieur Vieuxbois" (1837)
© *Tous les Albums de Töpffer, père de la BD*, 2014, Editions Fahrenheit 450.

The first page of "Les Amours de Monsieur Vieuxbois", by Rodolphe Töpffer, printed in 1837 in Geneva, Switzerland – © *Tous les Albums de Töpffer, père de la BD*, 2014, Editions Fahrenheit 450.

Its main character, "Mr Obadiah Oldbuck" is an American name given to Töpffer's fictional character, "Monsieur Vieuxbois", by Wilson and Co., a small publishing house in New York City. We know nothing of Wilson and Co. today, except that its offices moved from Nassau Street to Spruce Street, in Manhattan, circa 1846. Then it disappeared from all records.

Cover of an ulterior publishing "The Adventures of Mr. Obadiah Oldbuck"
(circa 1846), when Wilson é Co. publishing had moved its offices to Spruce Street.

On the cover of the first printing of "The Adventures of Mr. Obadiah Oldbuck", we read "Done with drawings by Timothy Crayon". Doubtless it is a pen name, because *crayon*, in French, means *pencil*.

We know about another pirated version of "Les Amours de Monsieur Vieuxbois", translated in English and printed in England circa 1846 by Tilt & Bogue, London. Here again, all Töpffer's works have been redrawn by an anonymous author, and the original title has been changed for "The Comical Adventures of Beau Ogleby". But the great originality of this other version is that it has been colorized, thus making it the first comic book in color ever published. As original printings of "The Adventures of Mr. Obadiah Oldbuck" are regularly found in United States and are not so rare, "The Comical Adventures of Beau Ogleby" is much more difficult to find and it remains an expensive collectible.

Title page of "The Comical Adventures of Beau Ogleby", circa 1846.

Finding a copy of "The Adventures of Mr. Obadiah Oldbuck" whose pages would be as clean as in this reprinting is impossible. After we digitalized several original copies, we selected the best pictures and restored them one by one, sketches, typography and frames separately. However, we abstained from going as far as recomposing the lines of the texts, and drawing some missing parts of the sketches owing to the poor printing quality common to all copies. Therefore, it is impossible to find an original printing of a better quality than this one.

Enjoy!

Mr. Oldbuck's first sight of his ladye-love.

Mr. Oldbuck beholds her vanishing in the distance,

Mr. Oldbuck in love.

He seeks to conquer the tender passion by study.

Mr. Oldbuck finding study ineffectual, tries music.

He discovers that all his efforts are in vain.

Looking from the window, Mr. Oldbuck espies his ladye-love.

He rushes to the street, but she has vanished.

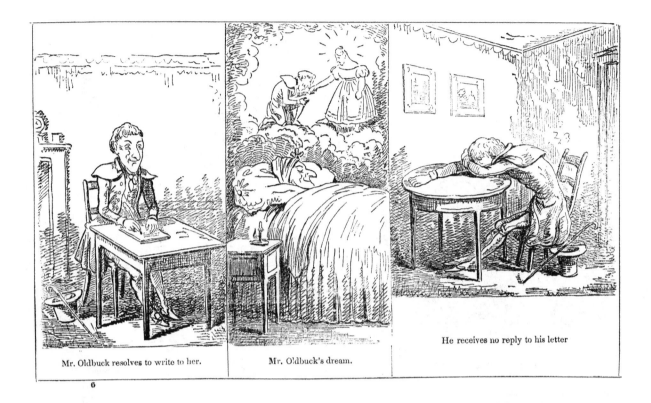

Mr. Oldbuck resolves to write to her.

Mr. Oldbuck's dream.

He receives no reply to his letter

Mr. Oldbuck, in despair, commits suicide. Fortunately the sword passes below his arm.

For eight-and-forty hours he believes himself dead.

He returns to life dying of hunger.

Third interview—declaration—sighs—hopes.

His beloved one leaves him—unhappy wretch!

Despair ! !

The remedy ! ! !

Second suicide of **Mr.** Oldbuck. Happily the rope is too long.

Eight-and-twenty hours afterwards, hearing the voice of his ladye-love in the street, Mr. Oldbuck forgets that he is hanged, and nearly strangles himself.

In his haste to reach his-ladye-love, he drags the beam after him.

Which rather annoys the good folks in the street.

Mr. Oldbuck almost overtakes his ladye-love,

Just as he reaches her, he is stopped by invidious fate.

Mr. Oldbuck wishes to return home, but can't.

He contrives ingeniously to overcome the difficulty.

Mr. Oldbuck sends for the doctor.

Mr. Oldbuck drinks ass's milk.

His physician recommending exercise, he purchases an Arabian courser.

Mr. Oldbuck on horseback.

Mr. Oldbuck is thrown.   His steed retreats to its stable.

Raising himself, Mr. Oldbuck perceives his ladye-love. She is not alone!

Duel between Mr. Oldbuck and his rival.

Having vanquished his adversary, Mr. Oldbuck declares his passion in presence of the parents of his beloved.

His suit being approved, Ms. Oldbuck returns home, and for three hours dances for joy.

At length their patience being exhausted the enraged neighbors rush in.

Mr. Oldbuck is imprisoned for midnight rioting.

The old folks on returning Mr. Oldbuck's visit, hear with astonishment that he is in prison.

His third suicide. The match being broken off, Mr. Oldbuck drinks hemlock. Luckily it is only vegetable soup.

For eight days Mr. Oldbuck believes himself dead,

The rats having gnawed the legs from the chair, he falls, and is restored to life.

Mr. Oldbuck turns over a new leaf.	He buys a watch-dog, and resolves to travel.	Being attacked by robbers, he hides himself and his horse behind a tree.

Stripped of every thing Mr. Oldbuck takes refuge in a cave.	He is discovered by a hermit, who condoles with him.	Mr. Oldbuck turns hermit.

Tired of seclusion, Mr. Oldbuck escapes in female disguise.

On his way he is accosted by a traveller on whom he recognises his own habiliments.

So at the next inn, he considers that to make an exchange is to commit no robbery.

Mr. Oldbuck rescues his horse from a ditch in which it has lain a fortnight.

He bewails the miserable condition of his steed.

Mr. Oldbuck finding his horse too weak to walk, treats him to a ride.

Arriving at a meadow, Mr. Oldbuck turns his horse into the rich pasture.

It soon recovers its flesh.

The rural solitude revives Mr. Oldbuck's flame.

He becomes sentimental.

And loves to roam.

His horse bursting with fat, Mr. Oldbuck is obliged to return home on foot.

On reaching home, Mr. Oldbuck finds a favorable letter from his ladyc-love.

He serenades his beloved object.

The elopement.

Mr. Oldbuck is recaptured by the monks and he and his beloved imprisoned in different cells.

| Fourth suicide of Mr. Oldbuck. | Fortunately in his descent he is caught by the index of a sun-dial. | He turns over a new leaf. | Mr. Oldbuck loses heart and falls ill. |

Profiting by his excessive thinness, Mr. Oldbuck introduces himself through the chimney which rather alarms his ladye-love.

They escape from their prison.

They continue to advance.

Their success all but certain.

But in fording the ditch, Mr. Oldbuck swallows more water than he relishes.

While his ladye-love dries herself in the sun, Mr. O dbuck amuses himself by drowning the porter who had pursued them.

They return home by water.

Taking their evening walk, the parents of the beloved one recognize their dear child at a distance.

Profiting by his situation, Mr. Oldbuck negotiates and obtains per-misssion to renew his suit.

The marriage is about to take place.

As he enters the church, Mr. Oldbuck remembers that he has shut up his dog at home, and goes back to let him out.

Returning to the church, he finds neither parents nor child!

Makes his will; exculpates his dog; charges the parents with his death; and requests the police to see to his funeral.

Fifth Suicide.   Mr. Oldbuck throws himself into the grand canal.

Happily two thieves fish him up for the sake of his bridal dress.   Being very determined, however, Mr. Oldbuck does not believe himself the less thoroughly drowned.

He is stripped and left naked on the bank.

Is found by the police, who take him away to be buried.

Is dug up by birds of prey, and returns to life.

Dressed in a winding-sheet Mr. Oldbuck returns home, but is discovered and pursued as a ghost.

Mr. Oldbuck reaches home, and almost frightens his heirs out of their wits.

He turns over a new leaf.

The heirs having complained to the police, Mr. Oldbuck is committed to prison.

36

Mr. Oldbuck pleads his own cause, but is sentenced to a years imprisonment.

He meditates an escape.

Having forced his way through the roof, he draws his dog up after him.

37

Mr. Oldbuck passes from the roof of the prison to that of a neighboring house.

Mr. Oldbuck sounds the chimney with his dog.

The chimney happens to be that of his beloved. Excessive fright of her parents. She recognises the dog and rushes to embrace it.

Unhappily while engaged in this tender duty, Mr. Oldbuck withdraws the cord.

| Mr. Oldbuck feels a great weight at the end of the string. | Just as they reach the top, the cord breaks. | Mr. Oldbuck is saved by falling into a street-lamp. |

| The loved one releases her father, who could not bring his mind to relax his hold of her. | Another releasement. The whole family meet on the roof and are surprised to find no one there. | Mr. Oldbuck, pursued by the police, disguises himself as an officer. |

Returning to the house of his ladye-love, Mr. Oldbuck learns that the whole family have been missing for three days.

Suspecting a plot, he sets out in search of his beloved.

At a loss to know what has happened to them, the family give themselves up to profound grief. At the end of four days they are discovered by a chimney-sweep.

Passing near some rich pasture, Mr. Oldbuck dismounts to take his horse by the head.

Meeting with one of the monks who imprisoned him, Mr. Oldbuck cuts off his beard.

He is pursued by a legion of enraged monks.

44

Mr. Oldbuck learns from the little chimney-sweep the fate of his ladye-love and her parents.

He mounts the sweep behind him to conduct him to their rescue.

He reaches the roof, comprehends the whole affair, and discovers his emaciated dog.

45

Mr. Oldbuck seeks to establish a correspondence with his ladye-love.

The parents of his beloved having, in their fright, changed their apartments, Mr. Oldbuck waits in vain eight days for a reply.

On the ninth he feels a light weight; in the intoxication of delight, he flatters himself that it is the beloved one herself!

46

A bitter disappointment.

The new comers taking the rope of Mr. Oldbuck for a pot-hook, hang their kettle upon it, and are dreadfully frightened to see it ascend the chimney.

47

Mr. Oldbuck's sensations on discovering his ladye-love at a window an the opposite side of the street.

Carried away by an excusable exultation, Mr. Oldbuck breaks a hole in the roof and disappears.

Falling into the room of a sleepy citizen, Mr. Oldbuck opens a communication with his ladye-love by means of the window.

Making a rope of the citizen's curtains, he descends without loosing sight of his beloved.

Midway, Mr. Oldbuck, by a well-directed leap, lands himself exactly in the chamber of his ladye-love.

Blissful moments, which amply repay all his exertions.

Even while engaged in making love, Mr. Oldbuck keeps his eyes about him.

Meantime the citizen, who had complained to the police, and having no intruder to deliver up, is arrested as a trickster or buffoon.

Second elopement. On this occasion Mr. Oldbuck conceals his beloved in a close carriage, with locked door to prevent every danger.

Mr. Oldbuck, espying a monk, spurs forward, unconscious of a little accident which has happened.

Mr. Oldbuck increasing his speed, advances at the rate of ten leagues an hour.

The carriage found by the diligence, is mounted on the roof.

The diligence being overset, the beloved one, favored by fate, floats resignedly on the water.

Discovering his loss, Mr. Oldbuck hastens to retrace his steps.

Excessive rage of Mr. Oldbuck, who, on reaching the banks of the river, sees his rival in possession of the carriage.

Mr. Oldbuck hesitates not to plunge into the river to swim in pursuit of his beloved.

In the mean time, the rival who had discovered and boarded the carriage, is carried by the current close to a great water-wheel.

Entangled by the water-wheel, the rival gets preciously duck-ed at every turn

Having reached the carriage, Mr. Oldbuck seats himself upon it, and steers with his hat.

Mr. Oldbuck seeks a flower-enamelled bank to land upon.

Meantime the rival continues to be soused at every turn.

Having landed on a flowery bank, Mr. Oldbuck draws the beloved one from the carriage.

Having become extremely thin, Mr. Oldbuck takes her to the mountains to drink milk.

The rival continues his evolutions.

For the sake of the health of his ladye-love, Mr. Oldbuck leads a pastoral life and takes the provisional name of Thyrsis.

The rival continues his aquatic amusement.

Mr. Oldbuck, under the assumed name of Thyrsis, milks the cow for his beloved.

Mr. Oldbuck, under the assumed name of Thyrsis, diverts his ladye-love with rustic dances.

When it begins to get cold, Mr. Oldbuck, under the assumed
name of Thyrsis, quits the high grounds to seek out a balmy
spot in the plains.

Meanwhile the waters decreasing, the river
leaves the carriage aground not far from the
convent.

The great wheel ceas-
ing to turn from the
same cause, the rival
returns to land

and dries himself in the sun.

The pastoral life having wonderfully fattened his ladye-love,
Mr. Oldbuck begins to get tired of it.

Having constructed a rustic palanquin, Mr. Oldbuck confides to two herdsmen the
task of conveying them home.

Mr. Oldbuck and his ladye-love having fallen asleep on the palanquin, are abandoned by the herdsmen.

The rival happening to pass, mounts the beloved one fast asleep on his donkey, and carries her off during Mr. Oldbuck's nap.

Excessive surprise of Mr. Oldbuck on awaking.

Pursuaded that the herdsmen are the thieves, he pursues them at the rate of five leagues an hour.

Once at full speed, Mr. Oldbuck, unable to stop or to turn aside, darts through a hay-rick.

Arriving at the same place, the rival dismounts his sleeping load and feeds his ass. The ass bites the foot of Mr. Oldbuck, who in vain shrieks aloud in the stack.

The rival going to sleep, the ass eats much hay, and Mr. Oldbuck begins to make his way out. Torments of jealousy.

Getting out, Mr. Oldbuck mounts his ladye-love on the ass, and makes off in double-quick time.

On awaking, the beloved asks, "Where are the herdsmen?"

Mr. Oldbuck continues his route, dragging the ass after him.

Crossing the territories of the monks, Mr. Oldbuck disguises himself as a miller, and passes his ladye-love off as a sack of flour.

The monks having right of toll, probe the sack, which collapses, uttering a frightful cry.

On seeing the sack begin to walk, the terrified monks, much to the satisfaction of Mr. Oldbuck, run off as fast as their legs can carry them.

The sack becoming untied, the monks return to the charge, and carry off the beloved one.

Mr. Oldbuck and his ladye-love having been tried and condemned, are led to the stake.

The fire having consumed the bottom of the posts, Mr. Oldbuck and his beloved make their escape.

They throw themselves into the river, and swim to the place where the carriage is stranded.

While his ladye-love dries herself in the sun, Mr. Oldbuck raises the carriage, and is nearly upset by the myriads of frogs disturbed by his intrusion.

Perceiving that he is pursued by the monks, Mr. Oldbuck hastens to lock himself and his ladye-love in the carriage, having first scattered some crowns on the ground.

The two monks, thinking from the crowns, that the carriage contains an immense treasure, dig a hole to hide it for themselves.

When it is deep enough, Mr. Oldbuck slips gently out of the carriage, pushes the monks into the hole, and throws the earth upon them.

Having carefully buried the monks up to the neck, Mr. Oldbuck politely takes leave of them, and makes off at his utmost speed.

The prolonged flight much fatigues the beloved one.

So Mr. Oldbuck gallantly takes the first opportunity which presents itself to procure a carriage.

Grand display of Mr. Oldbuck's strength.

Mr. Oldbuck's foot slipping, the wheelbarrow passes over him, and rushes down the hill with the speed of lightning.

The monks hearing a great noise behind them, are very uneasy, and cry out for help with all their might.

The noise waking up the rival, he hears the cries for help, hastens to see what is the matter, and recaptures the beloved one.

Mr. Oldbuck having somewhat recovered. pursues at full speed—Fifteen leagues in three hours !

Passing near the monks, he learns from them what has happened.   In gratitude Mr. Oldbuck releases them, and sets out at his utmost speed—twenty leagues in two hours !!

Night having arrived, the rival, for greater security, snatches some winks of sleep without leaving hold of the wheelbarrow

Mr. Oldbuck having discovered them, takes advantage of his rival's sleep, to tie his hands to the wheelbarrow ; and availing himself of this artifice, walks home at his ease.

On reaching home, Mr. Oldbuck turns over a new leaf.

Happy denouement of the history of Mr. Oldbuck.

[Egbert, Hovey & King, Printers.]

THE END

CPSIA information can be obtained
at www.ICGtesting.com
Printed in the USA
LVHW062006270621
691281LV00009B/884